FUN FACT FILE: SPORTS!

20 FUN FACTS ABOUT FOOTBALL

By Ryan Nagelhout

Gareth Stevens
PUBLISHING

Please visit our website, www.garethstevens.com. For a free color catalog of all our high-quality books, call toll free 1-800-542-2595 or fax 1-877-542-2596.

Cataloging-in-Publication Data

Nagelhout, Ryan.
20 fun facts about football / by Ryan Nagelhout.
p. cm. — (Fun fact file: sports!)
Includes index.
ISBN 978-1-4824-3974-8 (pbk.)
ISBN 978-1-4824-3975-5 (6-pack)
ISBN 978-1-4824-3976-2 (library binding)
1. Football — Juvenile literature. 2. Football — United States — Miscellanea — Juvenile literature. I. Nagelhout, Ryan. II. Title.
GV955.N34 2016
796.332'64021—d23

First Edition

Published in 2016 by
Gareth Stevens Publishing
111 East 14th Street, Suite 349
New York, NY 10003

Designer: Sarah Liddell
Editor: Ryan Nagelhout

Photo credits: Cover, p. 1 Eugene Onischenko/Shutterstock.com; p. 5 Wesley Hitt/Contributor/Getty Images Sport/Getty Images; p. 6 Bdcousineau/Wikimedia Commons; p. 7 The Washington Post/Contributor/The Washington Post/Getty Images; p. 8 GrapedApe/Wikimedia Commons; p. 9 Scewing/Wikimedia Commons; p. 10 Robert Ginn/Photolibrary/Getty Images; p. 11 Halvorsen brian/Wikimedia Commons; p. 12 Sporting News Archive/Contributor/Sporting News/Getty Images; p. 13 CBS Photo Archive/Contributor/CBS/Getty Images; p. 14 Al Pereira/Contributor/Getty Images Sport/Getty Images; p. 15 Otto Greule Jr/Stringer/Getty Images; p. 16 Rick Stewart/Stringer/Getty Images Sport/Getty Images; p. 17 Focus On Sport/Contributor/Focus On Sport/Getty Images; p. 18 New York Daily News Archive/Contributor/New York Daily News/Getty Images; p. 19 Brocreative/Shutterstock.com; p. 20 Rob Tringali/Contributor/SportsChrome/Getty Images; p. 21 Elsa/Staff/Getty Images Sport/Getty Images; p. 22 Kidwiler Collection/Contributor/Diamond Images/Getty Images; p. 23 John Biever/Contributor/Sports Illustrated/Getty Images; p. 24 George Rose/Stringer/Getty Images Sport/Getty Images; p. 25 Focus On Sport/Contributor/Getty Images Sport/Getty Images; p. 26 Steve Russell/Contributor/Toronto Star/Getty Images; p. 27 Rick Madonik/Contributor/Toronto Star/Getty Images; p. 29 Jamie Squire/Staff/Getty Images Sport/Getty Images.

Printed in the United States of America

CPSIA compliance information: Batch #CW16GS: For further information contact Gareth Stevens, New York, New York at 1-800-542-2595.

Contents

Words in the glossary appear in **bold** type the first time they are used in the text.

Football Fanatics

Baseball may be "America's pastime," but these days the National Football League (NFL) is the most popular sports league in the United States. It's fun to watch on TV and even more fun to watch from the stands!

But how much do you know about football? You may know that a field is called a gridiron, but do you know why? Did you know football is different in Canada? Let's see just how big of a football fanatic you are!

There's lots of history hidden inside the game of football.

FACT 1

The football "pigskin" was once really made of pig!

The first footballs were likely made from pig bladders. The bladder was tied up and inflated, or filled with air. Football historians say the football got its weird shape because the bladder couldn't get filled up all the way!

The official term for the shape of a football is a prolate spheroid—a round shape that has two pointed ends.

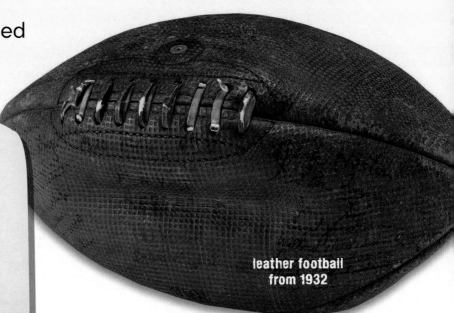

leather football from 1932

Today's kickers have special kicking footballs.

The "K-ball" came to the NFL in 1999 after the league found kickers were doctoring, or changing, balls to make them fly farther. K-balls are **slicker** than regular footballs. Kickers now rub them down before games so they can handle them better.

There were stories of kickers putting their footballs in microwave ovens, in the dryer, or even in steam rooms to change their shape!

FACT 3

The first "pro" football player was a man named Pudge Heffelfinger!

Heffelfinger was a guard at Yale University who was paid $500 by the Allegheny Athletic **Association** (AAA) in 1892. He helped the AAA beat the **rival** Pittsburgh Athletic Club, 4-0, by picking up a fumble and running 35 yards for the winning touchdown!

John Brallier

John Brallier was the first player to officially turn pro in 1895 when he was paid $10 and expenses to play for Latrobe YMCA against the Jeannette Athletic Club.

The king of Sweden told Jim Thorpe he was the greatest athlete in the world!

Thorpe was a star with the Canton Bulldogs and the Carlisle School of Indians team, an all–Native American group that toured the country in the 1910s. Thorpe also won the **decathlon** and **pentathlon** at the 1912 Olympic Games and played baseball and lacrosse.

Thorpe was one of the first 17 **inductees** into the Pro Football Hall of Fame in 1963.

FACT 5

The NFL was born in a city between Cleveland and Pittsburgh.

The American Professional Football Association was formed in Canton, Ohio, in 1920. It later became the NFL. The Canton Bulldogs were formed in 1904 and were one of the most successful early NFL teams, winning back-to-back NFL titles in 1922 and 1923.

The Bulldogs folded in 1926, but in 1963, the Football Hall of Fame opened in Canton and has grown ever since.

Could you imagine playing a football game inside a hockey rink? That's what the Bears had to do in 1932!

Chicago Stadium in 1930

FACT 6

The Chicago Bears once played inside due to bad weather!

In 1932, the Bears won the NFL championship against the Portsmouth Spartans inside Chicago Stadium. **Freezing** temperatures and a blizzard meant the game couldn't be played outside. The field was only 80 yards long and was 30 feet (9 m) narrower than a regular field!

FACT 7

Today's NFL is two different leagues that merged, or joined together.

In 1959, the American Football League (AFL) was started by Lamar Hunt. The AFL had eight teams, which were rivals with the NFL for fans and even players. Teams from the two leagues first played one another in Super Bowl I in 1967.

Lamar Hunt

The two leagues fully merged in 1970, with the NFL becoming the National Football **Conference** (NFC) and the AFL becoming the American Football Conference (AFC).

The AFL/NFL Merger

MINNESOTA • GREEN BAY • DETROIT • BUFFALO • BOSTON •
CHICAGO • CLEVELAND • NEW YORK • PITTSBURGH •
CINCINNATI • PHILADELPHIA • BALTIMORE •
DENVER • KANSAS CITY • ST. LOUIS • WASHINGTON •
OAKLAND • SAN FRANCISCO •
LOS ANGELES •
SAN DIEGO • DALLAS • ATLANTA •
HOUSTON • NEW ORLEANS • MIAMI

| ● NFL TEAMS | ● AFL TEAMS | ● TEAM IN BOTH LEAGES | ● TEAMS THAT WENT FROM THE NFL TO THE AFC |

Super Bowl I

What's in a Name?

Many football teams got their first name from baseball teams!

The New York Giants are named after the Major League Baseball (MLB) team that moved to San Francisco, California, in 1958. They were sometimes called the New York "Football" Giants to avoid **confusion**. The Pittsburgh Steelers were named the Pirates from 1933 to 1940.

The New York Jets were almost named the Dodgers, after an MLB team that once played in nearby Brooklyn.

Seattle Seahawks mascot, Blitz

In 1975, Seattle picked "Seahawks" out of more than 1,700 possible names sent in by fans, including Skippers, Pioneers, Lumberjacks, and Seagulls!

Some fans have picked their own team's name!

Many teams held **contests** to pick their team names. The Oakland Raiders, San Diego Chargers, Miami Dolphins, and many others were named by fans. The Jacksonville Jaguars were named by a fan even though jaguars aren't native to Jacksonville!

Football "Feets"

In 1982, a kicker won the league's Most Valuable Player (MVP) award.

Mark Mosley won the award playing for Washington in 1982. He made 20 of 21 field goals on the season, an amazing 95.2 **percent**! Mosley is the only kicker to ever win the MVP award.

Mark Mosley

The 1982 season was shortened to just a 9-game regular season because of a strike.

Tom Dempsey

A man with no toes once kicked a 63-yard field goal!

In 1970, Tom Dempsey kicked the then-record field goal in a 19-17 win for the New Orleans Saints over the Detroit Lions. Dempsey was born without toes on his right foot and without fingers on his right hand. The place-kicker played 11 seasons in the NFL!

In 2013, Denver kicker Matt Prater broke Dempsey's record with a 64-yard field goal.

The Forever Record

Frank Filchock

In 1939, Frank Filchock set a record that can never be broken!

The Washington quarterback threw a 99-yard touchdown pass to Andy Farkas on October 15, 1939, against Pittsburgh. The record has been matched more than 10 times since, but no one will ever throw a longer touchdown in the NFL.

It's not possible to throw a longer touchdown pass because the field is only 100 yards long and the ball can't be **snapped** on the goal line!

The Longest Touchdowns

LONGEST PUNT RETURN
Robert Bailey, Los Angeles Rams vs. New Orleans Saints
Oct. 23, 1994 (103 yards)

LONGEST KICKOFF RETURN
Cordarrelle Patterson, Minnesota Vikings vs. Green Bay Packers
Oct. 27, 2013 (109 yards)

LONGEST INTERCEPTION RETURN
Ed Reed, Baltimore Ravens vs. Philadelphia Eagles
Nov. 23, 2008 (107 yards)

LONGEST FUMBLE RETURN
Jack Tatum, Oakland Raiders vs. Green Bay Packers
Sept. 24, 1972
and Aeneas Williams, Arizona Cardinals vs. Washington Redskins
Nov. 5, 2000 (104 yards)

LONGEST MISSED FIELD GOAL RETURN
Antonio Cromartie, San Diego Chargers vs. Minnesota Vikings
Nov. 5, 2007 (109 yards)

END ZONE

END ZONE

10 20 30 40 50 40 30 20 10

A football field is called a gridiron because the yardage lines painted on it make it look like a gridiron, which is another name for the wire frame that holds food on a grill.

FACT 13

Brett Favre started 297 straight games at quarterback.

Favre played for the Green Bay Packers, New York Jets, Minnesota Vikings, and Atlanta Falcons over his 20-year career. From 1992 to 2010, the quarterback overcame broken bones and other **injuries** to play in every regular season game for nearly 19 straight seasons.

Favre's streak ended on December 12, 2010, when the Minnesota Vikings lost, 21-3, to the New York Giants.

In 2001, Favre was sacked by the New York Giants' Michael Strahan for the linebacker's record-setting 22.5 sack of the season.

FACT 14

Favre is the all-time leader in many "bad" quarterback stats.

Favre made the Pro Bowl 11 times and held many passing records, but he was sacked 525 times in his career, more than any other quarterback. He also had the most ever interceptions, 336, and quarterback fumbles, 166.

Bungling Bills

The Buffalo Bills once lost to the Miami Dolphins for an entire decade!

On September 7, 1980, the Bills beat the Dolphins, 17-7, at home to snap a 20-game losing streak against their rivals. Buffalo went "0 for the 70s" against Miami, their last win coming in 1969!

Fans in Buffalo stormed the field and tore down the goalposts after the game to celebrate the win!

Buffalo won AFL championships in 1964 and 1965, a year before the league winner got to play in the Super Bowl.

FACT 16

The Bills went to four straight Super Bowls... and lost all four!

The closest Buffalo came to a win was in Super Bowl 25 in 1990. Bills kicker Scott Norwood missed a 47-yard field goal with 8 seconds left, and the Giants won, 20-19. Buffalo then lost to Washington and twice to Dallas the next three seasons.

FACT 17

No team has ever had "home-field advantage" in a Super Bowl.

Two California teams came close, but the games were played in different stadiums. In 1980, the Los Angeles Rams played in Super Bowl 14 at the Rose Bowl in Pasadena, California, instead of their home field, Los Angeles Memorial Coliseum.

In 1985, the San Francisco 49ers played in Super Bowl 19, but the game was played in Stanford Stadium in nearby Stanford, California, and not their home field, Candlestick Park, in San Francisco.

The Paley Center had searched for tape of the first Super Bowl for more than 20 years!

Film footage of the first Super Bowl was lost until 2005!

Two networks—CBS and NBC—broadcast the game, but they both taped over copies of the game between the NFL's Green Bay Packers and the AFL's Kansas City Chiefs. The Paley Center for Media got a copy from a man who found a tape in a family member's attic!

Football Up North

FACT 19

A Canadian Football League (CFL) field is bigger than an NFL field.

An NFL playing field is 100 yards long and 53.3 yards wide. Midfield in the NFL is the 50-yard line. A CFL field is 110 yards long, which makes the 55-yard line midfield! A CFL field is also 65 yards wide.

NFL end zones are 10 yards deep. CFL end zones are twice as large, and the goalposts are actually in the end zone, which means the uprights sit on the goal line!

Calvillo even got his own postage stamp in Canada!

FACT 20

Anthony Calvillo has thrown for the most passing yards of all time!

Calvillo threw for 79,816 yards in his 20-year CFL career. He played for Las Vegas, Hamilton, and 16 seasons for the Montreal Alouettes. Montreal won the Grey Cup, the CFL's championship **trophy**, three times with Calvillo.

Changing the Game

Football has grown quickly into a major sport in America, but it's changed quite a bit along the way. Did you know that the touchdown wasn't always worth 6 points? It was actually worth 4 points until 1898, when it was changed to 5. It wasn't worth 6 points until 1912! A field goal was worth 4 points until 1909, when it was dropped to the 3-point play we know today.

As football continues to grow, new rules are added, and the game continues to change. Maybe the facts you know about the game now will soon be history!

The NFL is always looking to change rules to better the game. In 2015, they changed where the ball is snapped on an extra point from the 2-yard line to the 15-yard line!

Glossary

association: a group of people with a common interest

conference: a group of athletic teams

confusion: the state of being unclear

contest: an event where a winner is declared

decathlon: an athletic contest made up of 10 different track and field events

freezing: cold enough to turn from liquid to solid

inductee: a new member of a special group or club

injury: harm to the body that causes pain

pentathlon: an athletic contest made up of five different track and field events

percent: a measured part of a larger whole

rival: another team often competed against

slick: slippery or smooth

snap: to start a play in football

trophy: a prize given for winning

For More Information

Books

Bryant, Howard. *Legends: The Best Players, Games, and Teams in Football*. New York, NY: Philomel Books, 2015.

Buckley Jr., James. *Ultimate Guide to Football*. Santa Barbara, CA: Scholastic, 2010.

Rogers, Andy. *Who's Who of Pro Football: A Guide to the Game's Greatest Players*. North Mankato, MN: Capstone Press, 2016.

Websites

National Football League
nfl.com
Get schedules and more information about the NFL on its official site.

Pro Football Hall of Fame
profootballhof.com
Learn more about the greats of the game on the Hall of Fame website.

Pro Football Reference
pro-football-reference.com
Find facts, stats, and more about your favorite players and teams here.

Publisher's note to educators and parents: Our editors have carefully reviewed these websites to ensure that they are suitable for students. Many websites change frequently, however, and we cannot guarantee that a site's future contents will continue to meet our high standards of quality and educational value. Be advised that students should be closely supervised whenever they access the Internet.

Index